John Cotton

The New-England Primer Improved for the More Easy

Attaining the True Reading of English

To which is added The Assembly of Divines, and Mr. Cotton's Catechism

John Cotton

The New-England Primer Improved for the More Easy Attaining the True Reading of English
To which is added The Assembly of Divines, and Mr. Cotton's Catechism

ISBN/EAN: 9783337393397

Printed in Europe, USA, Canada, Australia, Japan

Cover: Foto ©Andreas Hilbeck / pixelio.de

More available books at **www.hansebooks.com**

The earliest information the publisher is *yet* able to collect, of the origin of the New England Primer, is contained in the following extract, from an Almanac now in the Library of the Massachusetts Historical Society, Boston.

IRA WEBSTER.

Boston, August 9th, 1844.

" AN

A L M A N A C K

Containing an Account of the *Cœleſtial Motions*, Aſpects, &c. For the year of the Chriſtian Empire, 1691.

By *Henry Newman*, Philomath.

Printed by *R. Pierce* for *Benjamin Harris* at the *London Coffee-Houſe in Boston*, 1691.

ADVERTISEMENT.

There is now in the Preſs, and will ſuddenly be extant, a Second Impreſſion of *the New England Primer enlarged*, to which is added, more *Directions for Spelling*: the *Prayer of* K. *Edward* the 6*th*. and *Verſes made by* Mr. Rogers *the Martyr, left as a Legacy to his Children.*

Sold by *Benjamin Harris*, at the *London Coffee-Houſe* in *Boſton*."

INTRODUCTION
TO THE PRESENT EDITION.

THE pious Baxter, who knew well the greater part of the Westminster Assembly of Divines, says, that the Christian world, since the days of the Apostles, never had a Synod of more excellent divines. The Assembly was convened in 1643; and was composed of *one hundred and twenty-one* divines, or presbyters, *thirty* lay assessors, and *five* commissioners from Scotland. It sat more than *five years and a half*.

Our Puritan Fathers brought the Shorter Catechism with them, across the ocean, and laid it on the same shelf with the family Bible. They taught it diligently to their children, every Sabbath. And while a few of their descendants, now in the *evening* of life, *remember* every question and answer; many, not yet advanced to life's *meridian*, can never *forget* when every Saturday *forenoon*, they had to take a regular catechising, in the common school, commencing with the a, b, c, *oaken-bench class*, "What is the chief end of man?"

If in this Catechism, the true and fundamental doctrines of the Gospel are expressed in fewer and better words, and definitions, than in any other summary, why ought we not *now* to *train up a child in the way he should go?*—why not *now*, put him in possession of the richest treasure that ever human wisdom and industry accumulated, to draw from?

HARTFORD, CONN.
PUBLISHED AND SOLD BY IRA WEBSTER. 1843
Stereotyped by R. H HOBBS.

ADVERTISEMENT.

A Society of ladies was formed in Boston, in the time of Mr. Whitefield, for improvement in personal piety, and to pray for the extension of the Redeemer's Kingdom. The Society met weekly for prayer, "reading some sound and serious book," singing, and other exercises adapted to "spiritual edification." "We also agree," say they, "once a quarter, to spend the day in prayer and other duties of religion, our special errand at the throne of grace to ask for the outpouring of the Spirit of God on us, our families, and the world of mankind."—"Once a quarter, the exercises shall be so shortened, as to have room to ask ourselves the Assembly's Shorter Catechism, that so we may keep in our minds that excellent form of sound words." This edition of the New England Primer, is a reprint and fac-simile of one of those owned and used by that Society.

A community of Boston ladies of "the olden time," enrolling the bright names and embodying the choice influences of the mothers of this Israel—the Masons and the Waterses of hallowed memory—assembled quarterly to refresh their minds from this Primer. The fact needs no comment.*

N. B. This statement is from a lady who was a member of the above Society, and from the documents of the Society in her possession.

---

* "*Most valuable of every thing, is the education and principles drawn from the mother's knee.*"—UPSHUR.

CERTIFICATES.

At the request of the publisher, the following certificate has been furnished by a gentleman who has given much attention to the subject of early School Books and Catechisms, in this country.

" The edition of the New England Primer, published in 1843 by Mr. Ira Webster, of Hartford, is a correct reprint of the oldest copy of that remarkable work, of which I have any knowledge ; perhaps the oldest copy now extant. All other reprints which I have seen, have been considerably altered—*modernized*—from the original.

 Cambridge, Oct. 20, 1849.   GEORGE LIVERMORE."

Communicated by the Rev. Thomas Williams :

" The edition of the New England Primer, which has been published by Mr. Ira Webster, of Hartford, in the year 1843, is the only genuine and correct edition of that valuable and wonderful book that has been to be obtained for many years. It is probably more than fifty years since there has been printed a complete and correct edition of the Primer, except the one printed by Mr. Webster. His edition is an exact copy of the Primer that was used by families and schools in my youth, sixty years ago, and I suppose it had been used for fifty or a hundred years before that time. The genuine copy of the Primer, on account of its antiquity, and its extensive usefulness in former years, has now become an object of interesting and beneficial curiosity."   THOMAS WILLIAMS.

 Plymouth, Massachusetts, June 23, *A. D.* 1844.

We, the subscribers, concur in the preceding statements.

          THOMAS ROBBINS,
          JOEL HAWES,
 Hartford, Oct. 30, 1849.   T. H. GALLAUDET.

The publisher of this edition, from one of 1777—(wishing to obtain information of still older copies,) would say that he has in his possession three Primers, two printed in Boston, 1770, 1777, and one in Providence, 1775, *all the same,* after the title page.

The Honorable JOHN HANCOCK, Efq;
Prefident of the *American* C o n g r e s s .

�֍✿✿✿✿✿✿✿✿✿✿✿✖✿✿✿✿✿✿✿✿✿✿

A Divine Song of Praiſe to G O D , for a Child,
by the Rev. Dr. W A T T S.

HOW glorious is our heavenly King,
  Who reigns above the Sky!
How ſhall a Child preſume to ſing
  His dreadful Majeſty!

How great his Power is none can tell,
  Nor think how large his Grace :
Nor men below, nor Saints that dwell
  On high before his Face.

Nor Angels that ſtand round the Lord,
  Can ſearch his ſecret will ;
But they perform his heav'nly Word,
  And ſing his Praiſes ſtill.

Then let me join this holy Train,
  And my firſt Off'rings bring ;
The eternal GOD will not diſdain
  To hear an Infant ſing.

My Heart reſolves. my Tongue obeys,
  And Angels ſhall rejoice,
To hear their mighty Maker's Praiſe,
  Sound from a feeble Voice.

✿✿✿✿✿✿✿✿✿✿✿✿✖✿✿✿✿✿✿✿✿✿✿

THE

NEW-ENGLAND

PRIMER

IMPROVED

For the more eaſy attaining the true
reading of Engliſh.

TO WHICH IS ADDED

The Aſſembly of Divines, and
Mr. COTTON's *Catechiſm.*

BOSTON:

Printed by EDWARD DRAPER, *at*
his Printing-Office, in *Newbury-*
Street, and *Sold* by JOHN BOYLE
in *Marlborough-Street.* 1777.

The young INFANT'S or CHILD'S morning Prayer.   *From* Dr. WATTS.

*A*LMIGHTY *God the Maker of every
Thing in Heaven and Earth; the Dark-
nefs goes away, and the Day light comes at thy
Command.   Thou art good and doeſt good continually.*

*I thank thee that thou haſt taken ſuch Care of
me this Night, and that I am alive and well this
Morning.*

*Save me, O God, from Evil, all this Day long,
and let me love and ſerve thee forever, for the
Sake of Jeſus Chriſt thy Son.*   AMEN.

The INFANT'S or young CHILD'S
Evening Prayer.   *From* Dr. WATTS.

O LORD *God who knoweſt all Things, thou
ſeeſt me by Night as well as by Day.*

*I pray thee for Chriſt's Sake, forgive me what-
ſoever I have done amiſs this Day, and keep me
all this Night, while I am aſleep.*

*I deſire to lie down under thy Care, and
to abide forever under thy Bleſſing, for thou
art a God of all Power and everlaſting Mercy.*
AMEN.

a b c d e f g h i j k l m
n o p q r ſ s t u v
w x y z &.

Vowels.

a e i o u y.

Conſonants.

b c d f g h j k l m n p q r ſ s t v w x z

Double Letters.

ct ff fi fl ffi ffl ſh ſi ſſi ſl ſſ ſt

Italick Letters.

Aa Bb Cc Dd Ee Ff Gg Hh
Ii Jj Kk Ll Mm Nn Oo Pp Qq
Rr Sſs Tt Uu Vv Ww Xx Yy Zz

Italick Double Letters.

ct ff fi ffi ſt ffl ſh ſi ſſ ſſi ſl. ſt.

Great Letters.

A B C D E F G H I J K L M N O

P Q R S T U W X Y Z.

Ab	eb	ib	ob	ub
ac	ec	ic	oc	uc
ad	ed	id	od	ud
af	ef	if	of	uf
ag	eg	ig	og	ug
aj	ej	ij	oj	uj
ak	ek	ik	ok	uk
al	el	il	ol	ul
am	em	im	om	um
an	en	in	on	un
ap	ep	ip	op	up
ar	er	ir	or	ur
as	es	is	os	us
at	et	it	ot	ut
av	ev	iv	ov	uv
ax	ex	ix	ox	ux
az	ez	iz	oz	uz

Eaſy

Eaſy Syllables, &c.

Ba	be	bi	bo	bu
ca	ce	ci	co	cu
da	de	di	do	du
fa	fe	fi	fo	fu
ga	ge	gi	go	gu
ha	he	hi	ho	hu
ja	je	ji	jo	ju
ka	ke	ki	ko	ku
la	le	li	lo	lu
ma	me	mi	mo	mu
na	ne	ni	no	nu
pa	pe	pi	po	pu
ra	re	ri	ro	ru
fa	fe	ſi	fo	fu
ta	te	ti	to	tu
va	ve	vi	vo	vu
wa	we	wi	wo	wu
ya	ye	yi	yo	yu
za	ze	zi	zo	zu

Words of one Syllable.

Age	all	ape	are
Babe	beef	beſt	bold
Cat	cake	crown	cup
Deaf	dead	dry	dull

Words of one Syllable.

Eat	ear	eggs	eyes
Face	feet	filth	foul
Gate	good	grafs	great
Hand	hat	head	heart
Ice	ink	ifle	jobb.
Kick	kind	kneel	know
Lamb	lame	land	long
Made	mole	moon	mouth
Name	night	noife	noon
Oak	once	one	ounce
Pain	pair	pence	pound
Quart	queen	quick	quilt
Rain	raife	rofe	run
Saint	fage	falt	faid
Take	talk	time	throat
Vain	vice	vile	view
Way	wait	wafte	would

Words of two Syllables.

Ab-fent	ab-hor	a-pron	au-thor
Ba-bel	be-came	be-guile	bold-ly
Ca-pon	cel-lar	con-ftant	cub-board
Dai-ly	de-pend	di-vers	du-ty
Ea-gle	ea-ger	en-close	e-ven
Fa-ther	fa-mous	fe-male	fu-ture
Ga-ther	gar-den	gra-vy	glo-ry

Words of two Syllables.

Hei-nous	hate-ful	hu-mane	hus-band
In-fant	in-deed	in-cence	i-fland
Ja-cob	jeal-ous	juf-tice	ju-lep
La-bour	la-den	la-dy	la-zy
Ma-ny	ma-ry	mo-tive	mu-fick

Words of three Syllables.

A-bu-fing	a-mend-ing	ar-gu-ment
Bar-ba-rous	be-ne-fit	beg-gar-ly
Cal-cu-late	can-dle-stick	con-foun-ded
Dam-ni-fy	dif-fi-cult	drow-fi-nefs
Ea-ger-ly	em-ploy-ing	evi-dence
Fa-cul-ty	fa-mi-ly	fu-ne-ral
Gar-de-ner	glo-ri-ous	gra-ti-tude
Hap-pi-ness	har-mo-ny	ho-li-nefs

Words of four Syllables.

A-bi-li-ty	ac-com-pa-ny	af-fec-ti-on
Be-ne-fi-ted	be-a-ti-tude	be-ne-vo-lent
Ca-la-mi-ty	ca-pa-ci-ty	ce-re-mo-ny
De-li-ca-cy	di-li-gent-ly	du-ti-ful-ly
E-dy-fy-ing	e-ver-laft-ing	e-vi-dent-ly
Fe-bru-a-ry	fi-de-li-ty	for-mi-da-bly
Ge-ne-ral-ly	glo-ri-fy-ing	gra-ci-ous-ly

Words of five Syllables.

A-bo-mi-na-ble   ad-mi-ra-ti-on
Be-ne-dic-ti-on   be-ne-fi-ci-al
Ce-le-bra-ti-on   con-fo-la-ti-on
De-cla-ra-ti-on   de-di-ca-ti-on
E-du-ca-ti-on   ex-hor-ta-ti-on
For-ni-ca-ti-on   fer-men-ta-ti-on
Ge-ne-ra-ti-on   ge-ne-ro-fi-ty

Words of fix Syllables.

A-bo-mi-na-ti-on   Gra-ti-fi-ca-ti-on
Be-ne-fi-ci-al-ly   Hu-mi-li-a-ti-on
Con-ti-nu-a-ti-on   I-ma-gi-na-ti-on
De-ter-mi-na-ti-on   Mor-ti-fi-ca-ti-on
E-di-fi-ca-ti-on   Pu-ri-fi-ca-ti-on
Fa-mi-li-a-ri-ty   Qua-li-fi-ca-ti-on

A Leſſon for Children.

Pray to God.   Call no ill names.
Love God.   Ufe no ill words.
Fear God.   Tell no lies.
Serve God.   Hate Lies.
Take not God's   Speak the Truth.
   Name in vain.   Spend your Time well
Do not Swear.   Love your School.
Do not Steal.   Mind your Book.
Cheat not in your play.   Strive to learn.
Play not with bad boys.   Be not a Dunce.

A	In A D A M's Fall We finned all.
B	Heaven to find, The Bible Mind.
C	Chrift crucify'd For finners dy'd.
D	The Deluge drown'd The Earth around.
E	E L I J A H hid By Ravens fed.
F	The judgment made F E L I X afraid.

G	As runs the Glass, Our Life doth pass.
H	My Book and Heart Must never part.
I	JOB feels the Rod,— Yet bleſſes GOD.
K	Proud Korah's troop Was ſwallowed up
L	LOT fled to *Zoar*, Saw fiery Shower On *Sodom* pour.
M	MOSES was he Who *Israel's* Hoſt Led thro' the Sea.

N N O A H did view
The old world & new

O Young O B A D I A S,
D A V I D, J O S I A S
All were pious.

P P E T E R deny'd
His Lord and cry'd.

Q Queen E S T H E R fues
And faves the *Jews.*

R Young pious R U T H,
Left all for 'Truth.

S Young S A M ' L dear.
The Lord did fear.

T Young T I M O T H Y
Learnt fin to fly.

U V A S T H I for Pride,
Was fet afide.

W Whales in the Sea,
GOD's Voice obey.

X X E R X E S did die,
And fo muft I.

Y While youth do chear
Death may be near.

Z Z A C C H E U S he
Did climb the Tree
Our Lord to fee.

WHO was the firſt man ?   *Adam.*
  Who was the firſt woman ?   *Eve.*
Who was the firſt Murderer ?   *Cain.*
Who was the firſt Martyr ?   *Abel.*
Who was the firſt Tranſlated ?   *Enoch.*
Who was the oldeſt Man ?   *Methuſelah.*
Who built the Ark ?   *Noah.*
Who was the Patienteſt Man ?   *Job.*
Who was the Meekeſt Man ?   *Moſes.*
Who led *Iſrael* into *Canaan ?*   *Joſhua.*
Who was the ſtrongest Man ?   *Sampſon.*
Who killed *Goliah ?*   *David.*
Who was the wiſeſt Man ?   *Solomon.*
Who was in the Whale's Belly ?   *Jonah.*
Who ſaves loſt Men ?   *Jeſus Chriſt.*
Who is *Jeſus Chriſt ?*   *The Son of God.*
Who was the Mother of *Chriſt ?*   *Mary.*
Who betrayed his Maſter ?   *Judas.*
Who denied his Maſter ?   *Peter.*
Who was the firſt Chriſtian Martyr ? *Stephen.*
Who was chief Apoſtle of the *Gentiles ? Paul.*

The Infant's Grace before and after Meat.

BLESS me, O Lord, and let my food
ſtrengther me to ſerve thee, for Jesus
Chriſt's ſake.   AMEN.

IDeſire to thank God who gives me food
to eat every day of my life. AMEN.

WHAT's right and good now ſhew me Lord, and lead me by thy grace and word. Thus ſhall I be a child of God, and love and fear thy hand and rod.

An Alphabet of Leſſons for Youth.

A Wiſe ſon maketh a glad father, but a fooliſh ſon is the heavineſs of his mother.

B Etter is a little with the fear of the Lord, than great treasure & trouble therewith.

C Ome unto Chriſt all ye that labor and are heavy laden and he will give you reſt.

D O not the abominable thing which I hate ſaith the Lord.

E Xcept a man be born again, he cannot ſee the kingdom of God.

F Ooliſhneſs is bound up in the heart of a child, but the rod of correction ſhall drive it far from him.

G ODLINESS is profitable unto all things, having the promiſe of the life that now is, and that which is to come.

H OLINESS becomes G O D ' s houſe for ever.

I T is good for me to draw near unto G O D.

KEEP thy heart with all diligence, for out of it are the iſſues of life.

LIARS ſhall have their part in the lake which burns with fire and brimſtone.

MANY are the afflictions of the right-ous, but the L o r d delivereth them out of them all.

NOW is the accepted time, now is the day of ſalvation.

OUT of the abundance of the heart the mouth ſpeaketh.

PRAY to thy Father which is in ſecret; and thy Father which ſees in ſecret ſhall reward thee openly.

QUIT you like men, be ſtrong, ſtand faſt in the faith.

REMEMBER thy Creator in the days of thy youth.

SEeſt thou a man wife in his own conceit, there is more hope of a fool than of him.

TRUST in God at all times, ye people, pour out your hearts before him.

UPON the wicked, God ſhall rain an horrible tempeſt.

WO to the wicked, it ſhall be ill with him, for the reward of his hands ſhall be given him.

E**X**HORT one another daily while it is called to day, left any of you be hardened thro' the deceitfulnefs of fin.

YOUNG men ye have overcome the wicked one.

Z Eal hath confumed me, becaufe thy enemies have forgotten the word of God.

The LORD's Prayer.

OUR Father which art in heaven, hallowed be thy name. Thy kingdom come. Thy will be done on earth as it is heaven. Give us this day our daily bread. And forgive us our debts as we forgive our debtors. And lead us not into temptation. But deliver us from evil. For thine is the kingdom, the power and the glory, forever. A M E N.

The C R E E D.

I BELIEVE in God the Father Almighty Maker of heaven and earth, and in Jefus Chrift his only Son our Lord, which was conceived by the Holy Ghoft, born of the Virgin Mary, fuffered under Pontius Pilate, was crucified, dead and buried. He defcended into hell. The third day he arofe again from the dead, and afcended into heaven, and fitteth on the right hand of God, the Father,

Almighty. From thence he fhall come to judge both the quick and the dead. I believe in the Holy Ghoft, the Holy Catholic Church, the communion of Saints, the forgivenefs of fins, the refurrection of the body, and the life everlafting. A M E N.

Dr. W A T T S's *Cradle Hymn.*

H U S H my dear, lie ftill and flumber,
   holy angels guard thy bed,
Heavenly bleflings without number,
   gently falling on thy head.
Sleep my babe, thy food and raiment
   houfe and home thy friends provide,
All without thy care or payment,
   all thy wants are well fupply'd.
How much better thou'rt attended,
   than the Son of God could be,
When from heaven he defcended,
   and became a child like thee.
Soft and eafy is thy cradle,
   coarfe and hard thy Saviour lay,
When his birth-place was a ftable,
   and his fofteft bed was hay.
Blefled Babe! what glorious features,
   fpotlefs fair, divinely bright!!
Muft he dwell with brutal creatures,

how could angels bear the fight!
Was there nothing but a manger,
    curſed finners could afford,
To receive the heavenly ſtranger ;
    did they thus affront their Lord.
Soft my child I did not chide thee,
    tho' my ſong may found too hard ;
'Tis thy mother fits befide thee,
    and her arms ſhall be thy guard.
Yet to read the ſhameful ſtory,
    how the Jews abus'd their King,
How they ferv'd the Lord of glory,
    makes me angry while I fing.
See the kinder ſhepherds round him,
    telling wonders from the ſky ;
There they fought him, there they found him.
    with his Virgin Mother by.
See the lovely Babe a dreſſing ;
    lovely Infant how he ſmil'd !
When he wept, the Mother's bleſſing
    sooth'd and huſh'd the holy child.
Lo ! he ſlumbers in his manger,
    where the horned oxen fed ;
Peace my darling here's no danger,
    here's no Ox a near thy bed.
'Twas to fave thee, child from dying,
    fave my dear from burning ſlame,

Bitter groans and endlefs crying,
  that thy bleft Redeemer came.
May'ft thou live to know and fear him,
  truft and love him all thy days !
Then go dwell for ever near him,
  fee his face and fing his praife.
I could give thee thoufand kiffes,
  hoping what I moft defire :
Not a mother's fondeft wifhes,
  can to greater joys afpire.

Verses *for Children.*

THOUGH I am young a little one,
  If I can fpeak and go alone,
Then I muft learn to know the Lord,
And learn to read his holy word.
'Tis time to feek to God and pray
For what I want for every day :
I have a precious foul to fave,
And I a mortal body have,
Tho' I am young yet I may die,
And haften to eternity :
There is a dreadful fiery hell,
Where wicked ones must always dwell :
There is a heaven full of joy,
Where godly ones must always ftay :
To one of thefe my foul must fly,
  As in a moment when I die :

2

When God that made me, calls me home,
I muſt not stay I muſt be gone.
He gave me life, and gives me breath,
And he can fave my foul from death,
By JESUS CHRIST my only Lord,
According to his holy word.
He clothes my back and makes me warm:
He faves my fleſh and bones from harm.
He gives me bread and milk and meat
And all I have that's good to eat.
When I am fick, he if he pleafe,
Can make me well and give me eafe:
He gives me fleep and quiet reſt,
Whereby my body is refreſh'd
The Lord is good and kind to me,
And very thankful I muſt be:
I muſt obey and love and fear him,
By faith in Chriſt I muſt draw near him.
I muſt not fin as others do,
Left I lie down in forrow too:
For God is angry every day,
With wicked ones who go aftray,
All finful words I must reftrain:
I muſt not take God's name in vain.
I muſt not work, I muſt not play,
Upon God's holy fabbath day.
And if my parents fpeak the word,

I muſt obey them in the Lord.
Nor ſteal, nor lie, nor ſpend my days,
In idle tales and fooliſh plays,
I muſt obey my Lord's commands,
Do ſomething with my little hands :
Remember my creator now,
In youth while time will it allow.
Young SAMUEL that little child,
He ſerv'd the Lord, liv'd undefil'd;
Him in his ſervice God employ'd,
While ELI's wicked children dy'd:
When wicked children mocking ſaid,
To a good man, *Go up bald head,*
God was diſpleas'd with them and ſent
Two bears which them in pieces rent,
I muſt not like theſe children vile,
Diſpleaſe my God, myſelf defile.
Like young ABIJAH, I muſt ſee,
That good things may be found in me,
Young King JOSIAH, that bleſſed **youth,**
He ſought the Lord and lov'd the truth;
He like a King did act his part,
And follow'd God with all his heart.
The little children they did ſing,
Hoſannahs to their heavenly King.
That bleſſed child young TIMOTHY,
Did learn God's word moſt heedfully.

It feem'd to be his recreation,
Which made him wife unto falvation :
By faith in Chrift which he had gain'd
With prayers and tears that faith unfeign'd.
Thefe good examples were for me ;
Like thefe good children I must be.
Give me true faith in Chrift my Lord,
Obedience to his holy word,
No word is in the world like thine,
There's none fo pure, fweet and divine.
From thence let me thy will behold,
And love thy word above fine gold.
Make my heart in thy ftatutes found,
And make my faith and love abound.
Lord circumcife my heart to love thee :
And nothing in this world above thee :
Let me behold thy pleafed face,
And make my foul to grow in grace,
And in the knowledge of my Lord
And Saviour Chrift, and of his word.

Another.

A W A K E, arife, behold thou haft,
Thy life a leaf, thy breath a blaft,
At night lay down prepar'd to have
Thy fleep, thy death, thy bed, thy grave.

L O R D if thou lengthen out my days,
Then let my heart fo fixed be,

That I may lengthen out thy praise,
And never turn afide from thee.
　So in my end I fhall rejoice,
In thy falvation joyful be ;
My foul fhall say with loud glad voice,
JEHOVAH who is like to thee ?
Who takeft the lambs into thy arms,
And gently leadeft thofe with young,
Who faveft children from all harms,
Lord, I will praife thee with my fong.
　And when my days on earth fhall end,
And I go hence and be here no more,
Give me eternity to fpend,
My G O D to praife forever more.

Another.

Good children muft,

Fear God all day,	Love Chrift alway,
Parents obey,	In fecret pray,
No falfe thing fay,	Mind little play,
By no fin ftray,	Make no delay,

In doing good.

Another.

I In the burying place may fee
　Graves fhorter there than I,
From death's arreft no age is free
　Young children too muft die.
My God may fuch an awful fight,

Awakening be to me!
Oh! that by early grace I might
For death prepared be.

Another.

NOW I lay me down to take my ſleep,
   I pray the Lord my ſoul to keep,
If I ſhould die before I wake,
I pray the Lord my ſoul to take.

Another.

FIrſt in the morning when thou doſt awake,
   To God for his grace thy petition make,
Some heavenly petition uſe daily to ſay,
That the God of heaven may bleſs thee alway.

Duty to God and our neighbour.

LOVE God with all your ſoul & ſtrength,
   With all your heart and mind;
And love your neighbour as yourſelf,
   Be faithful, juſt and kind.
Deal with another as you'd have
   Another deal with you:
What you're unwilling to receive,
   Be ſure you never do.

Our Saviour's Golden Rule.

BE you to others kind and true,
   As you'd have others be to you:
And neither do nor ſay to men,
   Whate'er you would not take again.

The Sum of the ten Commandments.

WITH all thy foul love God above,
  And as thyfelf thy neighbour love.
  · *Advice to Youth.* Eccle. xii.

NOW in the heat of youthful blood,
  Remember your Creator God;
Behold the months come haft'ning on,
When you fhall fay, *My joys are gone.*

  Behold the aged finner goes
Laden with guilt and heavy woes,
Down to the regions of the dead,
With endlefs curfes on his head.

  The duft returns to duft again,
The foul in agonies of pain,
Afcends to God not there to dwell,
But hears her doom and finks to hell.
Eternal King I fear thy name,
Teach me to know how frail I am,
And when my foul muft hence remove,
Give me a manfion in thy love.

Remember thy Creator in the days of thy youth.

CHILDREN your great Creator fear,
  To him your homage pay,
While vain employments fire your blood,
  And lead your thoughts aftray.
The due remembrance of his name
  Your first regard requires :

Till your breaſt glows with ſacred **love,**
  Indulge no meaner fires.
Secure his favour, and be wife,
  Before theſe cheerleſs days,
When age comes on, when mirth's **no more**
  And health and ſtrength decays.

Some proper Names of M E N *and* W O M E N,
  to teach Children to ſpell their own.

Men's Names.	Elias, Elizur, .
A Dam, Abel, Abraham,	Frederick, Francis,
Amos, Aaron,	Gilbert, Giles,
Abijah, Andrew,	George, Gamalial,
Alexander, Anthony,	Gideon, Gerſhom,
Bartholomew,	Heman, Henry,
Benjamin, Barnabas,	Hezekiah, Hugh,
Benoni, Barzillai,	John, Jonas, Iſaac,
Caleb, Cæſar,	Jacob, Jared, Job,
Charles, Christopher,	James, Jonathan,
Clement, Cornelius,	Iſrael, Joſeph,
David, Daniel,	Jeremiah, Joſhua,
Ephraim, Edward,	Joſiah, Jedediah,
Edmund, Ebenezer,	Jabez, Joel, Judah,
Elijah, Eliphalet,	Lazarus, Luke,
Eliſha, Eleazer,	Mathew, Michael,
Elihu, Ezekiel,	Moſes, Malachi,
	Nathaniel, Nathan,

Nicholas, Noadiah,
Nehemiah, Noah,
Obadiah, Ozias,
Paul, Peter, Philip,
Phineas, Peletiah,
Ralph, Richard,
Samuel, Sampſon,
Stephen, Solomon,
Seth, Simeon, Saul,

Shem, Shubal,
Timothy, Thomas,
Titus, Theophilus,
Uriah, Uzzah,
Walter, William,
Xerxes, Xenophon,
Zachariah, Zebdiel.
Zedekiah, Zadock,
Zebulon, Zebediah,

Women's Names.

A Bigail, Anne,
  Alice, Anna,
Bethiah, Bridget,
Cloe, Charity,
Deborah, Dorothy,
Dorcas, Dinah,
Damaris,
Elizabeth, Eſther,
Eunice, Eleanor,
Frances, Flora,
Grace, Gillet,
Hannah, Huldah,
Hepzibah,
Henrietta, Hagar.
Joanna, Jane,
Jamima, Iſabel,

Judith, Jennet,
Katharine, Katura,
Kezia, Lydia,
Lucretia, Lucy,
Louis, Lettice,
Mary, Margaret,
Martha, Mehitable,
Marcy, Merial,
Patience, Phylis,
Phebe, Priſcilla,
Rachel, Rebecca,
Ruth, Rhode, Roſe.
Sarah, Suſanna,
Tabitha, Tameſin,
Urſula,
Zipporah, Zibiah.

2*

MR. JOHN ROGERS, minister of the gospel in *London*, was the first martyr in Queen MARY's reign, and was burnt at *Smithfield, February* 14, 1554.—His wife with nine small children, and one at her breast following him to the stake; with which sorrowful sight he was not in the least daunted, but with wonderful patience died courageously for the gospel of JESUS CHRIST.

GIVE ear my children to my words
   Whom God hath dearly bought,
Lay up his laws within your heart,
   and print them in your thoughts.
I leave you here a little book
   for you to look upon,
That you may fee your father's face
   when he is dead and gone :
Who for the hope of heavenly things
   While he did here remain,
Gave over all his golden years
   to prifon and to pain.
Where I, among my iron bands,
   inclofed in the dark,
Not many days before my death,
   I did compofe this work :
And for example to your youth,
   to whom I wifh all good,
I fend you here God's perfect truth,
   and feal it with my blood.
To you my heirs of earthly things :
   which I do leave behind,
That you may read and underftand
   and keep it in your mind.
That as you have been heirs of that

that once fhall wear away,
You alfo may poffefs that part,
   which never fhall decay.
Keep always God before your eyes,
   with all your whole intent,
Commit no fin in any wife,
   keep his commandment.
Abhor that arrant whore of R o m e,
   and all her blafphemies,
And drink not of her curfed cup,
   obey not her decrees.
Give honor to your mother dear,
   remember well her pain,
And recompence her in her age,
   with the like love again.
Be always ready for her help,
   and let her not decay,
Remember well your father all,
   who would have been your ftay.
Give of your portion to the poor,
   as riches do arife,
And from the needy naked foul,
   turn not away your eyes :
For he that doth not hear the cry
   of thofe that ftand in need,
Shall cry himfelf and not be heard,
   when he does hope to fpeed.

If GOD hath given you increafe,
  and bleffed well your ftore,
Remember you are put in truft,
  and fhould relieve the poor.
Beware of foul and filthy luft,
  let fuch things have no place,
Keep clean your veffels in the LORD,
  that he may you embrace.
Ye are the temples of the LORD,
  for you are dearly bought,
And they that do defile the fame,
  fhall furely come to nought.
Be never proud by any means,
  build not your houfe too high,
But always have before your eyes,
  that you are born to die.
Defraud not him that hired is,
  your labour to fuftain,
But pay him ftill without delay,
  his wages for his pain.
And as you would that other men
  againft you fhould proceed,
Do you the fame to them again,
  when they do ftand in need.
Impart your portion to the poor,
  in money and in meat

And fend the feeble fainting foul,
  of that which you do eat.
Afk counfel always of the wife,
  give ear unto the end,
And ne'er refufe the fweet rebuke
  of him that is thy friend.
Be always thankful to the LORD,
  with prayer and with praife,
Begging of him to blefs your work,
  and to direct your ways.
Seek firft, I fay, the living GOD,
  and always him adore,
And then be fure that he will blefs,
  your bafket and your ftore.
And I befeech Almighty GOD,
  replenifh you with grace,
That I may meet you in the heavens,
  and fee you face to face.
And though the fire my body burns,
  contrary to my kind,
That I cannot enjoy your love
  according to my mind :
Yet I do hope that when the heavens
  fhall vanifh like a fcroll,
I fhall fee you in perfect fhape,
  in body and in foul.
And that I may enjoy your love,

and you enjoy the land,
I do befeech the living LORD,
  to hold you in his hand.
Though here my body be adjudg'd
  in flaming fire to fry,
My foul I truft, will ftraight afcend
  to live with GOD on high.
What though this carcafe fmart awhile
  what though this life decay,
My foul I hope will be with GOD,
  and live with him for aye.
I know I am a finner born,
  from the original,
And that I do deferve to die
  by my fore-father's fall :
But by our S A V I O U R ' s precious blood,
  which on the crofs was fpilt,
Who freely offer'd up his life,
  to fave our fouls from guilt :
I hope redemption I fhall have,
  and all who in him truft,
When I fhall fee him face to face,
  and live among the juft.
Why then fhould I fear death's grim look
  fince CHRIST for me did die,
For King and *Cæfar*, rich and poor,
  the force of death muft try

When I am chained to the ſtake,
   and ſagots girt me round,
Then pray the LORD my ſoul in heaven
   may be with glory crown'd.
Come welcome death the end of fears,
   I am prepar'd to die :
Thoſe earthly flames will ſend my ſoul
   up to the Lord on high.
Farewell my children to the world,
   where you muſt yet remain ;
The LORD of hoſts be your defence,
   'till we do meet again.
Farewell my true and loving wife,
   my children and my friends,
I hope in heaven to ſee you all,
   when all things have their end.
If you go on to ſerve the LORD,
   as you have now begun,
You ſhall walk ſafely all your days,
   until your life be done.
GOD grant you ſo to end your days,
   as he ſhall think it beſt,
That I may meet you in the heavens,
   where I do hope to reſt.

OUR days begin with trouble here,
   our life is but a ſpan,

And cruel death is always near,
  fo frail a thing is man.
Then fow the feeds of grace whilft young,
  that when thou com'ft to die,
Thou may'ft fing forth that triumph fong,
  Death where's thy victory.

Choice Sentences.

1. P R A Y i N G will make us leave finning, or finning will make us leave praying.

2. O u R weaknefs and inabilities break not the bond of our duties.

3. W H A T we are afraid to fpeak before men, we fhould be afraid to think before GOD.

Learn thefe four lines by heart.

H A V E communion with few,
  Be intimate with ONE,
Deal juftly with all,
Speak evil of none.

A G U R's Prayer.

R E M O V E far from me vanities and lies; give me neither poverty nor riches; feed me with food convenient for me: left I be full and deny thee, and fay, Who is the Lord? Or left I be poor and fteal and take the name of my GOD in vain.

T H E S H O R T E R

CATECHISM,

Agreed upon by the Reverend Affembly of
D I V I N E S at *Weftminfter.*

Queft. **W**•*H A T is the chief end of man ?*
Anf. Man's chief end is to
glorify God and enjoy him forever.

Q. 2. *What rule hath God given to di-*
rect us how we may glorify and enjoy him ?

A. The word of God which is contained
in the fcriptures of the old and new tefta-
ment is the only rule to direct us how we
may glorify God and enjoy him.

Q.3. *What do the fcriptures principally teach?*

A. The fcriptures principally teach what
man is to believe concerning God, and what
duty God requireth of man.

Q. 4. *What is God?*

A. God is a fpirit, infinite, eternal, and
unchangeable, in his being, wifdom, power,
holinefs, juftice, goodnefs and truth.

Q. 5. *Are there more Gods than one ?*

A. There is but ONE only, the living and true GOD.

Q. 6. *How many persons are there in the God-head?*

A. There are three perſons in the God-head, the Father, the Son, and the Holy Ghoſt, and theſe three are one GOD, the ſame in ſubſtance, equal in power and glory.

Q. 7. *What are the decrees of God?*

A. The decrees of God are his eternal purpoſe, according to the counſel of his own will, whereby for his own glory he hath fore-ordained whatſoever comes to paſs.

Q. 8. *How doth God execute his decrees?*

A. God executeth his decrees in the works of creation and providence.

Q. 9. *What is the work of creation?*

A. The work of creation is God's making all things of nothing by the word of his pow-er, in the ſpace of ſix days, and all very good.

Q. 10. *How did God create man?*

A. God created man male & female after his own image, in knowledge, righteouſneſs and holineſs, with dominion over the creatures

Q. 11. *What are God's works of providence?*

A. God's works of providence are his moſt holy, wiſe and powerful, preſerving & governing all his creatures and all their actions.

Q. 12. *What special act of providence did God exercise towards man in the estate wherein he was created ?*

A. When God had created man, he entered into a covenant of life with him upon condition of perfect obedience, forbidding him to eat of the tree of knowledge of good and evil, upon pain of death.

Q. 13. *Did our first parents continue in the estate wherein they were created ?*

A. Our first parents being left to the freedom of their own will, fell from the estate wherein they were created, by sinning against God.

Q. 14. *What is sin ?*

A. Sin is any want of conformity unto, or transgression of the law of God.

Q. 15. *What was the sin whereby our first parents fell from the estate wherein they were created ?*

A. The sin whereby our first parents fell from the estate wherein they were created, was their eating the forbidden fruit.

Q. 16, *Did all mankind fall in Adam's first transgression ?*

A. The covenant being made with *Adam*, not only for himself, but for his posterity,

all mankind defcending from him by ordinary generation, finned in him, and fell with
him in his firft tranfgreffion.

Q. 17. *Into what eftate did the fall bring
mankind?*

A. The fall brought mankind into an estate of fin and mifery.

Q. 18. *Wherein confifts the finfulnefs of
that eftate whereinto man fell?*

A. The finfulnefs of that eftate whereinto
man fell, confifts in the guilt of *Adam's* firft
fin, the want of original rightcousnefs, & the
corruption of his whole nature, which is commonly called original fin, together with all
actual tranfgreffions which proceed from it.

Q. 19. *What is the mifery of that eftate
whereinto man fell?*

A. All mankind by the fall loft communion with God, are under his wrath & curfe,
and fo made liable to the miferies in this life,
to death itfelf, & to the pains of hell forever.

Q. 20. *Did God leave all mankind to per-
ifh in the ftate of fin and mifery?*

A. God having out of his mere good
pleafure from all eternity elected fome to
everlafting life, did enter into a covenant of grace, to deliver them out of a ftate

of fin and mifery, and to bring them into a ftate of falvation by a Redeemer.

Q. 21. *Who is the Redeemer of God's elect?*

A. The only Redeemer of God's elect, is the Lord Jefus Chrift, who being the eternal Son of God, became man, and fo was, and continues to be God and man, in two diftinct natures, and one perfon forever.

Q. 22. *How did Chrift being the Son of God become man ?*

A. Chrift the Son of God became man by taking to himfelf a true body and a refonable foul, being conceived by the power of the Holy Ghoft, in the womb of the virgin *Mary*, and born of her, and yet without fin.

Q. 23. *What offices doth Chrift execute as our Redeemer ?*

A. Chrift as our Redeemer executes the office of a prophet, of a prieft, & of a king, both in his eftate of humiliation and exaltation.

Q. 24. *How doth Chrift execute the office of a prophet ?*

A. Chrift executeth the office of a prophet in revealing to us by his word and fpirit, the will of God for our falvation.

Q. 25. *How doth Chrift execute the office of a prieft ?*

A. Chriſt executeth the office of a prieſt in his once offering up himſelf a ſacrifice to ſatisfy divine juſtice, and reconcile us to God, and in making continual interceſſion for us.

Q. 26. *How doth Chriſt execute the office of a king?*

A. Chriſt executeth the office of a king in ſubduing us to himſelf, in ruling and defending us, and in reſtraining and conquering all his and our enemies.

Q 27 *Wherein did Chriſt's humiliation conſiſt?*

A. Chriſt's humiliation conſiſted in his being born and that in a low condition, made under the law, undergoing the miſeries of this life, the wrath of God, and the curſed death of the croſs, in being buried and continuing under the power of death for a time.

Q. 28. *Wherein conſiſts Chriſt's exaltation?*

A. Chriſt's exaltation conſiſteth in his riſing again from the dead on the third day, in aſcending up into heaven, and ſitting at the right hand of God the Father, and in coming to judge the world at the last day.

Q. 29. *How are we made partakers of the redemption purchased by Chriſt?*

A. We are made partakers of the redemption purchaſed by Chriſt by the effectual application of it to us by his holy Spirit.

Q. 30. *How doth the Spirit apply to us the redemption purchased by Christ?*

A. The Spirit applieth to us the redemption purchased by Christ, by working faith in us, and thereby uniting us to Christ in our effectual calling.

Q. 31. *What is effectual calling?*

A. Effectual calling is the work of God's Spirit, whereby convincing us of our sin and misery, enlightening our minds in the knowledge of Christ, and renewing our wills, he doth persuade and enable us to embrace Jesus Christ, freely offered to us in the gospel.

Q. 32. *What benefits do they that are effectually called partake of in this life?*

A. They that are effectually called do in this life partake of justification, adoption, and sanctification, and the several benefits which in this life do either accompany or flow from them.

Q. 33. *What is justification?*

A. Justification is an act of God's free grace, wherein he pardoneth all our sins, and accepteth us as righteous in his sight, only for the righteousness of Christ imputed to us, and received by faith alone.

Q. 34. *What is adoption?*

A. Adoption is an act of God's free grace whereby we are received into the number, and have a right to all the privileges of the fons of God.

Q. 35. *What is fanctification?*

A. Sanctification is the work of God's free grace, whereby we are renewed in the whole man, after the image of God, and are enabled more and more to die unto fin, and live unto righteoufnefs.

Q. 36. *What are the benefits which in this life do accompany or flow from juftification, adoption and fanctification?*

A. The benefits which in this life do accompany or flow from juftification, adoption and fanctification, are affurance of God's love, peace of confcience, joy in the holy Ghoft, increase of grace, and perfeverance therein to the end.

Q. 37. *What benefits do believers receive from Chrift at their death?*

A. The fouls of believers are at their death made perfect in holinefs, and do immediately pafs into glory, and their bodies being ftill united to Chrift do reft in their graves 'till the refurrection.

Q. 38. *What benefits do believers receive from Chrift at the resurrection?*

A. At the refurrection believers being raifed up to glory, shall be openly acknowledged and acquitted in the day of judgment, and made perfectly bleffed in the full enjoyment of God to all eternity.

Q. 39. *What is the duty which God requires of man?*

A. The duty which God requires of man, is obedience to his revealed will.

Q. 40. *What did God at firft reveal to man for the rule of his obedience?*

A. The rule which God at firft revealed to man for his obedience was the moral law.

Q. 41. *Where is the moral law fummarily comprehended?*

A. The moral law is fummarily comprehended in the ten commandments.

Q. 42. *What is the fum of the ten commandments?*

A. The fum of the ten commandments is, to love the Lord our God with all our heart, with all our foul, with all our ftrength, and with all our mind, and our neighbour as ourfelves.

Q. 43. *What is the preface to the ten*

commandments ?

A. The preface to the ten command-ments is in thefe words, *I am the Lord thy God which have brought thee out of the land of* Egypt, *and out of the houfe of bondage.*

Q. 44. *What doth the preface to the ten commandments teach us ?*

A. The preface to the ten commandments teacheth us, that becaufe God is the Lord, and our God and Redeemer, therefore we are bound to keep all his commandments.

Q. 45. *Which is the first commandment ?*

A. The firft commandment is, *Thou fhalt have no other Gods before me.*

Q. 46. *What is required in the firft com-mandment ?*

A. The firft commandment requireth us to know and acknowledge God, to be the only true God, and our God, and to wor-fhip and glorify him accordingly.

Q. 47. *What is forbidden in the first com-mandment ?*

A. The firft commandment forbiddeth the denying or not worfhipping and glorify-ing the true God, as God, and our God, and the giving that worfhip and glory to any other which is due to him alone.

Q. 48. *What are we especially taught by these words* (before me) *in the first commandment?*

A. Thefe words (*before me*) in the firft commandment, teach us, that God who feeth all things, taketh notice of and is much difpleafed with the fin of having any other God.

Q. 49. *Which is the fecond commandment?*

A. The fecond commandment is, *Thou fhalt not make unto thee any graven image, or the likeness of any thing that is in heaven above, or that is in the earth beneath, or that is in the water under the earth; thou fhalt not bow down thyfelf to them nor serve them, for I the Lord thy God am a jealous God, vifiting the iniquities of the fathers upon the children, unto the third and fourth generation of them that hate me and fhewing mercy unto thoufands of them that love me & keep my commandments.*

Q. 50. *What is required in the fecond commandment?*

A. The fecond commandment requireth the receiving, obferving, & keeping pure and entire all fuch religious worfhip and ordinances, as God hath appointed in his word.

Q. 51. *What is forbidden in the fecond commandment?*

A. The ſecond commandment forbiddeth the worſhipping of God by images or any other way not appointed in his word.

Q. 52. *What are the reaſons annexed to the ſecond commandment?*

A. The reaſons annexed to the ſecond commandment, are God's ſovereignty over us, his propriety in us, and the zeal he hath to his own worſhip.

Q. 53. *Which is the third commandment?*

A. The third commandment is, *Thou ſhalt not take the name of the Lord thy God in vain, for the Lord will not hold him guiltleſs, that taketh his name in vain.*

Q. 54. *What is required in the third commandment?*

A. The third commandment requireth the holy and reverent uſe of God's names, titles, attributes, ordinances, word and works.

Q. 55. *What is forbidden in the third commandment?*

A. The third commandment forbiddeth all profaning or abuſing of any thing whereby God maketh himſelf known.

Q. 56. *What is the reaſon annexed to the third commandment?*

A. The reaſon annexed to the third commandment is, That however the breakers of this commandment may eſcape puniſhment from men, yet the Lord our God will not ſuffer them to eſcape his righteous judgment.

Q. 57. *Which is the fourth commandment?*

A. The fourth commandment is, *Remember the ſabbath day to keep it holy, ſix days ſhalt thou labor and do all thy work, but the ſeventh day is the ſabbath of the Lord thy God, in it thou ſhalt not do any work, thou nor thy ſon, nor thy daughter, thy man-ſervant, nor thy maid ſervant, nor thy cattle, nor the ſtranger that is within thy gates, for in ſix days the Lord made heaven and earth, the ſea and all that in them is, and reſted the ſeventh day, wherefore the Lord bleſſed the ſabbath day and hallowed it.*

Q. 58. *What is required in the fourth commandment?*

A. The fourth commandment requireth, the keeping holy to God ſuch ſet times as he hath appointed in his word, expreſſly one whole day in ſeven to be an holy Sabbath to himſelf.

Q. 59. *Which day of the ſeven hath God appointed to be the weekly ſabbath?*

A. From the beginning of the world, to the refurrection of Chrift, God appointed the feventh day of the week to be the weekly fabbath, and the firft day of the week ever fince to continue to the end of the world, which is the Chriftian Sabbath.

Q. 60. *How is the fabbath to be fanctified ?*

A. The fabbath is to be fanctified by an holy refting all that day, even from fuch worldly employments and recreations as are lawful on other days, and fpending the whole time in public and private exercifes of God's worfhip, except fo much as is to be taken up in the works of neceffity and mercy.

Q. 61. *What is forbidden in the fourth commandment ?*

A. The fourth commandment forbiddeth, the omiffion or carelefs performance of the duties required, and the profaning the day by idlenefs,or doing that which is in itfelf finful, or by unneceffary thoughts, words or works, about worldly employments or recreations.

Q. 62. *What are the reafons annexed to the fourth commandment ?*

A. The reafons annexed to the fourth commandment, are God's allowing us fix days of the week for our own employment, his challenging a special propriety in the feventh, his own example,& his bleffing the fabbath day.

Q. 63. *Which is the fifth commandment?*

A. The fifth commandment is, *Honor thy father and thy mother, that thy days may be long upon the land which the Lord thy God giveth thee.*

Q. 64. *What is required in the fifth commandment?*

A. The fifth commandment requireth the preferving the honor, and performing the duties belonging to every one in their feveral places and relations, as fuperiors, inferiors, or equals.

Q. 65. *What is forbidden in the fifth commandment?*

A. The fifth commandment forbiddeth the neglecting of, or doing any thing against the honour and duty which belongeth to every one in their feveral places and relations.

Q. 66. *What is the reason annexed to the fifth commandment?*

A. The reason annexed to the fifth commandment is a promife of long life and profperity, (as far as it fhall ferve for God's glory and their own good) to all fuch as keep this commandment.

Q. 67. *Which is the fixth commandment?*

A. The fixth commandment is, *Thou fhalt not kill.*

Q. 68. *What is required in the fixth commandment ?*

A. The fixth commandment requireth all lawful endeavors to preferve our own life, and the life of others.

Q. 69. *What is forbidden in the fixth commandment ?*

A. The fixth commandment forbiddeth the taking away of our own life, or the life of our neighbour unjuftly, and whatfoever tendeth thereunto.

Q. 70. *Which is the feventh commandment ?*

A. The feventh commandment is, *Thou fhalt not commit adultery.*

Q. 71. *What is required in the feventh commandment ?*

A. The feventh commandment requireth the prefervation of our own and our neighbor's chastity, in heart, speech & behaviour.

Q. 72. *What is forbidden in the feventh commandment ?*

A. The feventh commandment forbiddeth all unchafte thoughts, words and actions.

Q. 73. *Which is the eighth commandment ?*

A. The eighth commandment is, *Thou*

3*

ſhalt not ſteal.

Q. 74. *What is required in the eighth commandment ?*

A. The eighth commandment requireth the lawful procuring & furthering the wealth and outward eſtate of ourſelves and others.

Q. 75. *What is forbidden in the eighth commandment ?*

A. The eighth commandment forbiddeth whatſoever doth, or may unjuſtly hinder our own or our neighbour's wealth or outward eſtate.

Q. 76. *Which is the ninth commandment ?*

A. The ninth commandment is, *Thou ſhalt not bear false witneſs againſt thy neighbour.*

Q. 77. *What is required in the ninth commandment ?*

A. The ninth commandment requireth the maintaining and promoting of truth between man & man, & of our own & our neighbor's good name, eſpecially in witneſs bearing.

Q. 78. *What is forbidden in the ninth commandment ?*

A. The ninth commandment. forbiddeth whatſoever is prejudicial to truth, or injurious to our own or our neighbor's good name.

Q. 79. *Which is the tenth commandment ?*

A. The tenth commandment is, *Thou ſhalt not covet thy neighbour's houſe, thou ſhalt not covet thy neighbour's wife, nor his man-ſervant, nor his maid-ſervant, nor his ox, nor his aſs, nor any thing that is thy neighbour's.*

Q. 80. *What is required in the tenth commandment?*

A. The tenth commandment requireth full contentment with our own condition, with a right and charitable frame of ſpirit towards our neighbour, and all that is his.

Q. 81. *What is forbidden in the tenth commandment?*

A. The tenth commandment forbiddeth all diſcontentment with our own eſtate, envying or grieving at the good of our neighbour, and all inordinate motions and affections to any thing that is his.

Q. 82. *Is any man able perfectly to keep the commandments of God?*

A. No mere man ſince the fall is able in this life perfectly to keep the commandments of God, but daily doth break them in thought, word and deed.

Q. 83. *Are all tranſgreſſions of the law equally heinous?*

A. Some ſins in themſelves, and by reafon of feveral aggravations, are more heinous in the fight of God than others.

Q. 84. *What doth every fin deferve?*

A. Every fin deferves God's wrath & curfe both in this life, and that which is to come.

Q. 85. *What doth God require of us that we may efcape his wrath and curfe due to us for fin?*

A. To efcape the wrath and curfe of God due to us for fin, God requireth of us faith in Jefus Chrift, repentance unto life, with the diligent ufe of all outward means whereby Chrift communicateth to us the benefits of redemption. Q. 86. *What is faith in Jefus Chrift?*

A. Faith in Jefus Chrift is a faving grace whereby we receive & reft upon him alone for falvation as he is offered to us in the gofpel.

Q. 87. *What is repentance unto life?*

A. Repentance unto life is a faving grace, whereby a finner out of the true fenfe of his fin and apprehenfion of the mercy of God in Chrift, doth with grief and hatred of his fin turn from it unto God, with full purpofe of and endeavours after new obedience.

Q. 88. *What are the outward and ordinary means whereby Chrift communicateth to us the benefits of redemption?*

A. The outward and ordinary means where

by Chriſt communicateth to us the benefits of redemption, are his ordinances, eſpecially the word, ſacraments and prayer ; all which are made effectual to the elect for ſalvation.

Q. 89. *How is the word made effectual to ſalvation ?*

A. The ſpirit of God maketh the reading, but eſpecially the preaching of the word an effectual means of convincing and converting ſinners, and of building them up in holineſs and comfort, through faith unto ſalvation.

Q. 90. *How is the word to be read and heard that it may become effectual to ſalvation?*

A. That the word may become effectual to ſalvation, we must attend thereunto with diligence, preparation and prayer, receive it with faith and love, lay it up in our hearts, and practice it in our lives.

Q. 91 *How do the ſacraments become effectual means of ſalvation ?*

A. The ſacraments become effectual means of ſalvation not from any virtue in them or in him that doth adminiſter them, but only by the bleſſing of Chriſt, and the working of the Spirit in them that by faith receive them.

Q. 92. *What is a ſacrament ?*

A. A ſacrament is an holy ordinance inftituted by Chrift, wherein by fenfible figns, Chrift & the benefits of the new covenant are reprefented fealed and applied to believers.

Q. 93. *What are the facraments of the New Teftament?*

A. The facraments of the New Tefta-ment are baptifm and the Lord's fupper.

Q. 94. *What is baptism?*

A. Baptifm is a facrament wherein the wafh-ing of water in the name of the Father and of the Son and of the Holy Ghoft, doth fignify and feal our ingrafting into Chrift and par-taking of the benefits of the covenant of grace, & our engagements to be the Lord's.

Q. 95. *To whom is baptism to be administered?*

A. Baptifm is not to be adminiftered to any that are out of the vifible church, till they profefs their faith in Chrift, and obedience to him, but the infants of fuch as are mem-bers of the vifible church are to be baptized.

Q. 96. *What is the Lord's fupper?*

A. The Lord's fupper is a facrament, wherein by giving and receiving bread and wine according to Chrift's appointment, his death is fhewed forth, and the worthy recei-vers are not after a corporal and carnal man-ner, but by faith made partakers of his body and blood, with all his benefits, to their fpiritual nourifhment and growth in grace.

Q. 97. *What is required in the worthy receiving the Lord's fupper?*

A. It is required of them that would worthily partake of the Lord's fupper, that they examine themfelves of their knowledge to difcern the Lord's body, of their faith to feed upon him, of their repentance, love and new obedience, left coming unworthily, they eat and drink judgment to themfelves.

Q. 98. *What is prayer?*

A. Prayer is an offering up of our defires to God for things agreeable to his will, in the name of Chrift, with confeffion of our fins, & thankful acknowledgment of his mercies.

Q. 99. *What rule hath God given for our direction in prayer?*

A. The whole word of God is of ufe to direct us in prayer but the fpecial rule of direction is that form of prayer which Chrift taught his difciples commonly called, *The Lord's Prayer.*

Q. 100. *What doth the preface of the Lord's prayer teach us?*

A. The preface of the Lord's prayer which is *Our Father which art in heaven,* teacheth us, to draw near to God with all holy reverence and confidence, as children to a father, able and ready to help us, and that we fhould pray with and for others.

Q.101. *What do we pray for in the first petition?*

A. In the firſt petition, which is, *Hallowed be thy name,* we pray that God would enable us and others to glorify him in all that whereby he makes himſelf known, and that he would diſpoſe all things to his own glory.

Q. 102. *What do we pray for in the ſecond petition?*

A. In the ſecond petition, which is, *Thy kingdom come,* we pray that ſatan's kingdom may be deſtroyed, the kingdom of grace may be advanced, ourſelves and others bro't into it, and kept in it, and that the kingdom of glory may be haſtened.

Q. 103. *What do we pray for in the third petition?*

A. In the third petition, which is, *Thy will be done on earth as it is in heaven,* we pray that God by his grace would make us able and willing to know, obey and ſubmit to his will in all things, as the angels do in heaven.

Q. 104. *What do we pray for in the fourth petition?*

A. In the fourth petition, which is, *Give*

us this day our daily bread, we pray, that of God's free gift we may receive a competent portion of the good things of this life, and enjoy his bleffing with them.

Q. 105. *What do we pray for in the fifth petition ?*

A. In the fifth petition, which is, *And forgive us our debts as we forgive our debtors*, we pray that God for Chrift's fake, would freely pardon all our fins, which we are the rather encouraged to afk, becaufe by his grace we are enabled from the heart to forgive others.

Q. 106. *What do we pray for in the fixth petition ?*

A. In the fixth petition, which is, *And lead us not into temptation, but deliver us from evil*, we pray that God would either keep us from being tempted to fin, or fupport and deliver us when we are tempted.

Q. 107. *What doth the conclufion of the Lord's prayer teach us ?*

A. The conclufion of the Lord's prayer, which is, *For thine is the kingdom, and the power, and the glory, forever*, A M E N, teacheth us, to take our encouragement in prayer from God only, and in our prayers to praife him, afcribing kingdom, power and glory to him, and in teſtimony of our deſire and aſſurance to be heard, we ſay, A M E N.

Bleſſed are they that do his commandments that they may have right to the tree of life, and may enter in through the gates into the city. Rev. xxii. 14.

❋❋❋❋❋❋❋❋❋❋❋❋❋❋❋❋❋❋❋❋❋❋

SPIRITUAL MILK

F O R

American B A B E S,

Drawn out of the Breaſts of both *Teſtaments*

for their Souls Nouriſhment.

By J O H N   C O T T O N.

Q *WHAT hath God done for you?*
    A. God hath made me, he keepeth me, and he can ſave me.

Q. *What is God?*
A. God is a Spirit of himſelf & for himſelf.

Q. *How many Gods be there?*
A. There is but one God in three Perſons, the Father, and the Son, and the Holy Ghoſt

Q. *How did God make you?*
A. In my firſt parents holy and righteous.

Q. *Are you then born holy and righteous*.

A. No, my firſt father ſinned and I in him.

Q. *Are you then born a ſinner?*

A. I was conceived in ſin, & born in iniquity

Q. *What is your birth ſin?*

A. Adam's ſin imputed to me, and a corrupt nature dwelling in me.

Q. *What is your corrupt nature?*

A. My corrupt nature is empty of grace, bent unto ſin, only unto ſin, and that continually.

Q. *What is ſin?*

A. Sin is a tranſgreſſion of the law.

Q. *How many commandments of the law be there?*   A. Ten.

Q. *What is the first commandment?*

A. Thou ſhalt have no other Gods before me.

Q. *What is the meaning of this commandment?*

A. That we ſhould worſhip the only true God, and no other beſides him.

Q. *What is the ſecond commandment?*

A. Thou ſhalt not make to thyſelf any graven image, &c.

Q. *What is the meaning of this commandment?*

A. That we ſhould worſhip the only true God, with true worſhip, ſuch as he hath ordained, not ſuch as man hath invented.

Q. *What is the third commandment?*

A. Thou fhalt not take the name of the Lord thy God in vain.

Q. What is meant by the name of God?

A. God himfelf & the good things of God, whereby he is known as a man by his name, and his attributes, worfhip, word and works.

Q. What is it not to take his name in vain?

A. To make ufe of God & the good things of God to his glory, and our own good, not vainly, not irreverently, not unprofitably.

Q. Which is the fourth commandment?

A. Remember that thou keep holy the fabbath day.

Q. What is the meaning of this commandment?

A. That we fhould reft from labor, and much more from play on the Lord's day, that we may draw nigh to God in holy duties.

Q. What is the fifth commandment?

A Honor thy father and thy mother, that thy days may be long in the land which the Lord thy God giveth thee.

Q. What are meant by father and mother?

A. All our fuperiors whether in family, fchool, church and common wealth.

Q. What is the honor due unto them?

A. Reverence, obedience, and (when I am able) recompence.

Q. *What is the fixth commandment?*

A. Thou fhalt do no murder.

Q. *What is the meaning of this commandment?*

A. That we fhould not fhorten the life or health of ourfelves or others, but preferve both

Q. *What is the feventh commandment?*

A. Thou fhalt not commit adultery.

Q. *What is the fin here forbidden?*

A. To defile ourfelves or others with unclean lufts.

Q. *What is the duty here commanded?*

A. Chaftity to poffefs our veffels in holinefs and honor.

Q. *What is the eighth commandment?*

A. Thou fhalt not fteal.

Q. *What is the ftealth here forbidden?*

A. To take away another man's goods without his leave, or to fpend our own without benefit to ourfelves or others.

Q. *What is the duty here commanded?*

A. To get our goods honeftly, to keep them fafely, and fpend them thriftily.

Q. *What is the ninth commandment?*

A. Thou fhalt not bear falfe witnefs againft thy neighbour.

Q. *What is the fin here forbidden?*

A. To lie falfely, to think or fpeak **untru**ly of ourfelves or others.

Q. What is the duty here required ?

A. Truth and faithfulnefs.

Q. What is the tenth commandment ?

A. Thou fhalt not covet, &c.

Q. What is the coveting here forbidden ?

A. Luft after the things of other men, and want of contentment with our own.

Q. Whether have you kept all thefe commandments ?

A. No, I and all men are finners.

Q. What are the wages of fin ?

A. Death and damnation.

Q. How then look you to be faved ?

A. Only by Jefus Chrift.

Q. Who is Jefus Chrift ?

A. The eternal Son of God, who for our fakes became man, that he might redeem & fave us.

Q. How doth Chrift redeem and fave us ?

A. By his righteous life, and bitter death, and glorious refurrection to life again.

Q. How do we come to have a part & fellowfhip with Chrift in his death & refurrection?

A. By the power of his word and fpirit, which brings us to him, and keeps us in him.

Q. What is the word ?

A. The holy fcriptures of the prophets and apoftles, the old and new teftament, the law and gofpel.

Q. How doth the miniftry of the law bring you toward Chrift?

A. By bringing me to know my fin, and the wrath of God, againft me for it.

Q. What are you hereby the nearer to Chrift?

A. So I come to feel my curfed eftate and need of a Saviour.

Q. How doth the miniftry of the Gofpel help you in this curfed eftate?

A. By humbling me yet more, and then raifing me out of this eftate.

Q. How doth the miniftry of the Gofpel humble you yet more?

A. By revealing the grace of the Lord Jefus in dying to fave finners, and yet convincing me of my fin in not believing on him, and of my utter infufficiency to come to him, and fo I feel myfelf utterly loft.

Q. How doth the miniftry of the gospel raife you up out of this loft eftate to come to Chrift?

A. By teaching me the value and virtue of the death of Chrift, and the riches of his grace to loft finners by revealing the promife of grace to fuch, and by miniftring the Spirit of grace to apply Chriſt, and his promiſe of grace unto myſelf, and to keep me in him.

Q. *How doth the Spirit of grace apply Chriſt & his promiſe grace unto you and keep you in him?*

A. By begetting in me faith to receive him, prayer to call upon him, repentance to mourn after him, and new obedience to ſerve him.

Q. *What is faith ?*

A. Faith is the grace of the Spirit, whereby I deny myſelf, and believe on Chriſt for righteouſneſs and ſalvation.

Q. *What is prayer ?*

A. It is calling upon God in the name of Chriſt by the help of the Holy Ghoſt, accor ding to the will of God.

Q. *What is repentance ?*

A. Repentance is a grace of the Spirit, whereby I loath my ſins, and myſelf for them and confeſs them before the Lord, and mourn after Chriſt for the pardon of them, and for grace to ſerve him in newneſs of life.

Q. *What is the newneſs of life, or new obedience?*

A. Newneſs of life is a grace of the Spirit, whereby I forſake my former luſt & vain company, and walk before the Lord in the light of his word, and in the communion of ſaints.

Q. *What is the communion of ſaints ?*

A. It is the fellowſhip of the church in the bleſſings of the covenant of grace, and the ſeals thereof.   Q. *What is the church?*

A. It is a congregation of ſaints joined together in the bond of the covenant, to wor-ſhip the Lord, and to edify one another in all his holy ordinances.

Q, *What is the bond of the covenant by which the church is joined together?*

A. It is the profeſſion of that covenant which God has made with his faithful people, to be a God unto them, and to their ſeed.

Q. *What doth the Lord bind his people to in this covenant?*

A. To give up themſelves & their ſeed firſt to the Lord to be his people,&then to the el-ders & brethren of the church to ſet forward the worſhip of God & their mutual edification.

Q. *How do they give up themſelves and their ſeed to the Lord?*

A. By receiving thro' faith the Lord & his covenant to themſelves,&to their ſeed & ac-cordingly walking themſelves & training up their children in the ways of the covenant.

Q.*How do they give up themſelves and their ſeed to the elders and brethren of the church?*

A. By confeſſing of their ſins, and profeſ-

4

fion of their faith, and of their fubjection to
the gofpel of Chrift; and fo they and their
feed are received into the fellowfhip of the
church and the feals thereof.

Q. *What are the feals of the covenant now
in the days of the gofpel?*

A. Baptifm and the Lord's Supper. ·

Q. *What is done for you in baptifm?*

A. In baptifm the wafhing with water is
a fign and feal of my wafhing in the blood
and fpirit of Chrift, and thereby of my ingrafting into Chrift, of the pardon and clean-
fing of my fins, of my raifing up out of afflictions, and alfo of my refurrection from the
dead at the laft day.

Q. *What is done for you in the Lord's fupper?*

A. In the Lord's fupper, the receiving of the
bread broken and the wine poured out is a fign
and feal of my receiving the communion of
the body of Chrift broken for me, and of his
blood fhed for me, and thereby of my growth
in Chrift, and the pardon and healing of my
fins, of the fellowfhip of the Spirit, of my
ftrengthening and quickening in grace, and
of my fitting together with Chrift on his
throne of glory at the laft judgment.

Q. *What was the refurrection from the*

dead, which was fealed up to you in baptism ?

A. When Chrift fhall come in his laft judgment, all that are in their graves fhall rife again, both the juft and unjuft.

Q. What is the judgment, which is fealed up to you in the Lord's supper ?

A. At the laft day we fhall all appear before the judgment feat of Chrift, to give an account of our works, and receive our reward according to them.

Q. What is the reward that fhall then be given?

A. The righteous fhall go into life eternal, and the wicked fhall be caft into everlafting fire with the Devil and his angels.

A DIALOGUE *between* CHRIST, YOUTH, *and the* Devil.　　　YOUTH.

THofe days which God to me doth fend,
　　In pleafure I'm refolv'd to fpend ;
Like as the birds in th' lovely spring,
Sit chirping on the bough, and fing ;
Who ftraining forth thofe warbling notes,
Do make fweet mufic in their throats,
So I refolve in this my prime,
In fports and plays to fpend my time.
Sorrow and grief I'll put away,
Such things agree not with my day :

From clouds my morning fhall be free ,
And nought on earth fhall trouble me.
I will embrace each fweet delight,
This earth affords me day and night :
Though parents grieve and me correct,
Yet I their counsel will reject.

Devil.

   The refolution which you take,
Sweet youth it doth me merry make.
If thou my counsel wilt embrace,
And fhun the ways of truth and grace,
And learn to lie, and curfe and swear.
And be as proud as any are ;
And with thy brothers wilt fall out,
And fifters with vile language flout ·
Yea, fight and fcratch, and alfo bite,
Then in thee I will take delight.
If thou wilt but be rul'd by me,
An artift thou fhalt quickly be,
In all my ways which lovely are,
Ther'e few with thee who fhall compare.
Thy parents always difobey ;
Don't mind at all what they do fay :
And alfo pout and fullen be,
And thou fhalt be a child for me.
When others read, be thou at play,
Think not on God, don't sigh nor pray

Nor be thou such a silly fool,
To mind thy book or go to school;
But play the truant; fear not I
Will straitway help you to a lie,
Which will excuse thee from the same,
From being whipp'd and from all blame;
Come bow to me, uphold my crown,
And I'll thee raise to high renown.

YOUTH.

These motions I will cleave unto,
And let all other counsels go;
My heart against my parents now,
Shall harden'd be, and will not bow:
I won't submit at all to them,
But all good counsels will condemn,
And what I list that do will I,
And stubborn be continually.

CHRIST.

Wilt thou, O youth make such a choice,
And thus obey the devil's voice!
Curst sinful ways wilt thou embrace,
And hate the ways of truth and grace?
Wilt thou to me a rebel prove?
And from thy parents quite remove
Thy heart also? Then shalt thou see,
What will e'er long become of thee.
Come, think on God, who did thee make,

4*

And at his prefence dread and quake,
Remember him now in thy youth,
And let thy foul take hold of truth:
The Devil and his ways defy,
Believe him not, he doth but lie:
His ways feem fweet, but youth beware,
He for thy foul hath laid a fnare.
His fweet will into bitter turn,
If in thofe ways thou ftill wilt run,
He will thee into pieces tear,
Like lions which moft hungry are.
Grant me thy heart, thy folly leave,
And from this lion I'll thee fave;
And thou fhalt have fweet joy from me,
Which fhall laft to eternity.

YOUTH.

My heart fhall chear me in my youth,
I'll have my frolicks in good truth,
What e'er feems lovely in mine eye.
Myfelf I cannot it deny.
In my own ways I ftill will walk,
And take delight among young folk,
Who fpend their days in joy and mirth,
Nothing like that I'm fure on earth:
Thy ways, O Chrift! are not for me,
They with my age do not agree.
If I unto thy laws fhould cleave,

No more good days then fhould I have.
CHRIST.
Woul'ft thou live long and good days fee
Refrain from all iniquity :
True good alone doth from me flow,
It can't be had in things below.
Are not my ways, O youth! for thee,
Then thou fhalt never happy be ;
Nor ever fhall thy foul obtain,
True good, whilft thou doft here remain
YOUTH.
To thee, O Chrift, I'll not adhere,
What thou fpeak'st of does not appear
Lovely to me I cannot find,
'Tis good to fet or place my mind
On ways whence many forrows fpring
And to the flefh fuch croffes bring,
Don't trouble me, I muft fulfil,
My flefhly mind, and have my wil'.
CHRIST.
Unto thyfelf then I'll thee leave,
That Satan may thee wholly have :
Thy heart in fin fhall harden'd be,
And blinded in iniquity.
And then in wrath I'll cut thee down
Like af the grafs and flowers mown ·
And to thy woe thou fhalt efpy,

Childhood and youth are vanity;
For all fuch things I'll make thee know
To judgment thou fhall come alfo.
In hell at laft thy foul fhall burn,
When thou thy finful race haft run.
Confider this, think on thy end
Left God do thee in pieces rend.

YOUTH.

Amazed, Lord! I now begin,
O help me and I'll leave my fin:
I tremble, and do greatly fear,
To think upon what I do hear.
Lord! I religious now will be,
And I'll from Satan turn to thee.

Devil.

Nay, foolifh youth, don't change thy mind,
Unto fuch thoughts be not inclin'd.
Come, cheer up thy heart, roufe up, be **glad**.
There is no hell; why art thou fad?
Eat, drink, be merry with thy friend,
For when thou dieft, that's thy laft end.

YOUTH.

Such thoughts as thefe I can't receive,
Becaufe God's word I do believe;
None fhall in this deftroy my faith,
Nor do I mind what Satan faith.

Devil.

Although to thee herein I yield,
Yet e'er long I shall win the field.
That there's a heaven I can't deny,
Yea, and a hell of misery :
That heaven is a lovely place
I can't deny ; 'tis a clear case ;
And easy 'tis for to come there,
Therefore take thou no further care,
All human laws do thou observe,
And from old customs never swerve ;
Do not oppose what great men say,
And thou shalt never go astray.
Thou may'st be drunk, and swear and curse,
And sinners like thee ne'er the worse ;
At any time thou may'st repent ;
'Twill serve when all thy days are spent.

CHRIST.

Take heed or else thou art undone ;
These thoughts are from the wicked One,
Narrow's the way that leads to life,
Who walk therein do meet with strife.
Few shall be saved, young man know,
Most do unto destruction go.
If righteous ones scarce saved be,
What will at last become of thee !
Oh ! don't reject my precious call,
Lest suddenly in hell thou fall ;

Unlefs you foon converted be,
God's kingdom thou fhalt never fee.

YOUTH.

Lord, I am now at a great ftand :
If I fhould yield to thy command,
My comrades will me much deride,
And never more will me abide.
Moreover, this I alfo know,
Thou can'ft at laft great mercy fhow.
When I am old, and pleafure gone,
Then what thou fay'ft I'll think upon.

CHRIST.

Nay, hold vain youth, thy time is fhort,
I have thy breath, I'll end thy fport;
Thou fhalt not live till thou art old,
Since thou in fin art grown fo bold.
I in thy youth grim death will fend,
And all thy fports fhall have an end.

YOUTH.

I am too young, alas to die,
Let death fome old grey head efpy.
O fpare me, and I will amend,
And with thy grace my foul befriend,
Or elfe I am undone alas,
For I am in a woful cafe.

CHRIST.

When I did call, you would not hear,

But didſt to me turn a deaf ear;
And now in thy calamity,
I will not mind nor hear thy cry;
Thy day is paſt, begone from me,
Thou who didſt love iniquity,
Above thy ſoul and Saviour dear;
Who on the croſs great pains did bear,
My mercy thou didſt much abuſe,
And all good counſel didſt refuſe,
Juſtice will therefore vengeance take,
And thee a ſad example make.

YOUTH.

O ſpare me, Lord, forbear thy hand,
Don't cut me off who trembling ſtand,
Begging for mercy at thy door,
O let me have but one year more.

CHRIST.

If thou ſome longer time ſhould have,
Thou wouldſt again to folly cleave:
Therefore to thee I will not give,
One day on earth longer to live.

Death.

Youth, I am come to fetch thy breath,
And carry thee to th' ſhades of death,
No pity on thee can I ſhow,
Thou haſt thy God offended ſo.
Thy ſoul and body I'll divide,

Thy body in the grave I'll hide,
And thy dear foul in hell muſt lie
With Devils to eternity.

The concluſion.

Thus end the days of woful youth,
Who won't obey nor mind the truth;
Nor hearken to what preachers ſay,
But do their parents diſobey.
They in their youth go down to hell,
Under eternal wrath to dwell.
Many don't live out half their days,
For cleaving unto ſinful ways.

The late Reverend and Venerable Mr. N A-
T H A N I E L C L A P, *of* Newport *on* Rhode
Iſland; *his Advice to children.*

GOOD children ſhould remember daily,
God their Creator, Redeemer, and
Sanctifier; to believe in, love and ſerve him;
their parents to obey them in the L O R D;
their bible and catechiſm; their baptiſm;
the L O R D's day; the L O R D's death and re-
ſurrection; their own death and reſurrecti-
on; and the day of judgment, when all that
are not fit for heaven muſt be ſent to hell.
And they ſhould pray to G O D in the name
of C H R I S T, for ſaving grace